BATMAN

THE ANIMATED SERIES GUIDE

LONDON, NEW YORK, TORONTO,
MELBOURNE, MUNICH, AND DELHI

Editor Alastair Dougall
Designer Robert Perry
Art Director Mark Richards
Publishing Manager Cynthia O'Neill Collins
Category Publisher Alex Kirkham
Production Nicola Torode

First American Edition, 2003
03 04 05 06 07 10 9 8 7 6 5 4 3 2 1

Published in the United States by DK Publishing, Inc.
375 Hudson Street, New York, New York 10014

DK Publishing, Inc. offers special discounts for bulk purchases for sales promotions or premiums. Specific, large-quantity
needs can be met with special editions, including personalized covers, excerpts of existing guides, and corporate imprints.
For more information, contact Special Markets Department, DK Publishing, Inc., 375 Hudson Street, New York, NY 10014
Fax: 800-600-9098.

Library of Congress Cataloging-in-Publication Data

Beatty, Scott, 1969-
  Batman, the animated series guide / by Scott Beatty.-- 1st American
ed.
     p. cm. -- (DC animated series guides)
Includes index.
  ISBN 0-7894-9580-5 (hardcover)
  1. Batman, the animated series (Television program) I. Title. II. Series.
  PN1992.77.B343B43 2003
  791.45'72--dc21

                              2003001172

Reproduced by Media Development and Printing, UK
Printed and bound in Italy by L.E.G.O.

Visit DC Comics online at www.dccomics.com or at keyword DC Comics on America Online.

see our complete product line at
www.dk.com

BATMAN

THE ANIMATED SERIES GUIDE

Written by Scott Beatty
Batman created by Bob Kane

DK

CONTENTS

GREETINGS FROM GOTHAM	5	RĀ'S AL GHŪL	32
BATMAN	6	TALIA	33
LAIR OF THE BAT	8	MAD HATTER	34
NIGHTWING	10	SCARECROW	35
ROBIN	12	MR. FREEZE	36
ALFRED	14	CLAYFACE	37
COMMISSIONER GORDON	16	MASK OF THE PHANTASM	38
BATGIRL	17	THE RIDDLER	40
CITIZENS OF GOTHAM	18	BANE	41
THE JOKER	20	MAN-BAT	42
HARLEY QUINN	22	VENTRILOQUIST	43
TWO-FACE	24	ROGUES' GALLERY	44
CATWOMAN	26		
POISON IVY	28	GAZETTEER	46
PENGUIN	30	INDEX	47
KILLER CROC	31	ACKNOWLEDGMENTS	48

GREETINGS FROM GOTHAM

Be warned. You are about to enter the most dangerous metropolis in the world. Gotham City is overrun by vice and villainy. But in the midst of crime and corruption, hope comes in the form of a Dark Knight. His name is Batman… and together with a small band of costumed companions and police allies, he wages war on crime to liberate Gotham from the forces of evil.

From his secret underground base, the Batcave, the Dark Knight is joined by Nightwing, Robin, and Batgirl for this bold battle against the Joker, Two-Face, Poison Ivy, and so many other raging rogues!

Gotham isn't the safest place to visit. But with the Batman watching over you from above, you *just* might make it out alive…

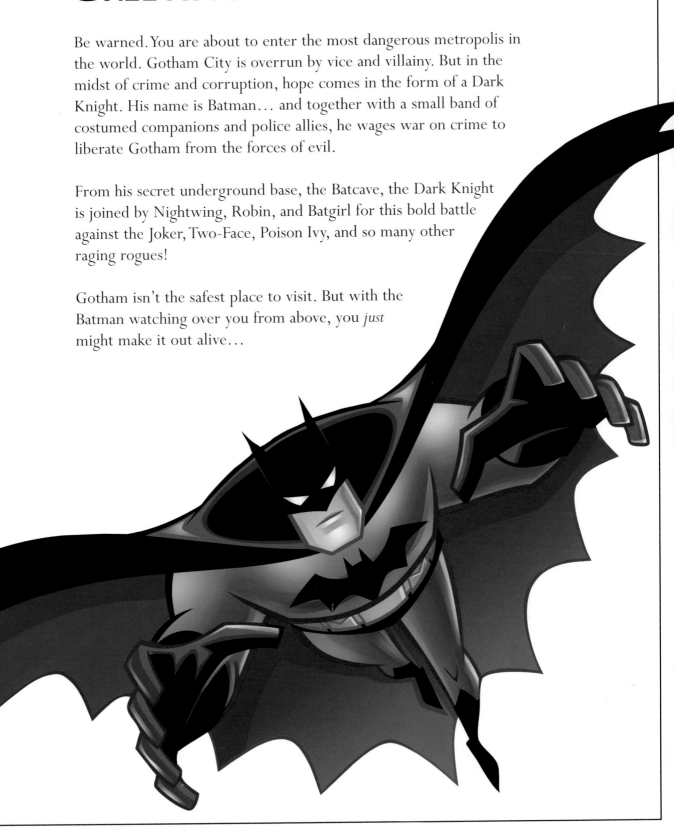

BATMAN

Bruce Wayne's happy childhood ended in tragedy when a ruthless killer shot his parents in Gotham City's "Crime Alley." Young Bruce made a vow to avenge their deaths. He would turn himself into a living weapon and wage an all-out war on crime as the Dark Knight Detective, Batman!

THOMAS AND MARTHA Wayne were killed on their way home from a late-night screening of *The Mask of Zorro*.

BRUCE WAYNE

Batman's alter ego is Bruce Wayne, the head of Wayne Enterprises. Except for a few trusted friends, no one knows that bored billionaire Bruce is actually the crime busting Caped Crusader!

BAT DATA

• Because his parents were shot and killed, Batman never uses a gun.

• The Dark Knight's preferred weapon is the Batarang, which is thrown like a boomerang!

THE DARK KNIGHT fights tirelessly to protect the innocent victims of injustice. He will not allow any children to suffer or be orphaned as he was at such an early age.

Batman's cape is bulletproof and flame-resistant.

Batman's mask has night-vision lenses.

His Utility Belt is packed with equipment to counter crime.

Batman's steel-toed boots have rubber soles for extra grip.

WAYNE'S WORLD

Bruce's ancestral home is luxurious Wayne Manor, a sprawling estate located on hundreds of acres north of Gotham and just outside the city limits.

SHADOW OF THE BAT

At first, Bruce wore a plainclothes disguise to fight crime. But to frighten the fight out of criminals, he soon adopted a costume modeled in the terrifying image of a bat!

BATMAN may be outnumbered by Gotham's hordes of hooligans, but he'll never give up. The unstoppable Dark Knight is determined to chase every last criminal out of town!

LAIR OF THE BAT

Buried far below stately Wayne Manor is the Dark Knight's underground base, the Batcave! This high-tech haunt is where Batman plans his war on crime. The Batcave is filled from stalagmite to stalactite with all the necessary weapons to wage an all-out assault on arch-villainy!

CAVE DWELLERS

Only butler Alfred Pennyworth and a few close friends know that an antique grandfather clock in Bruce Wayne's study conceals the entrance to the Batcave!

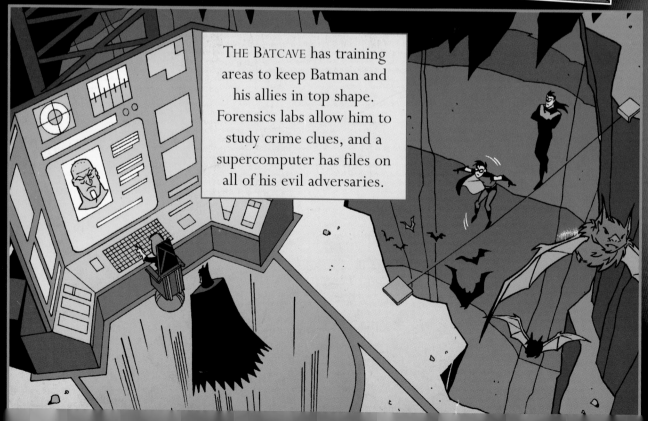

THE BATCAVE has training areas to keep Batman and his allies in top shape. Forensics labs allow him to study crime clues, and a supercomputer has files on all of his evil adversaries.

Batcycle

Batplane

BAT-VEHICLES ready for launch from the Batcave include Nightwing and Robin's turbo-charged Batcycles. A hangar holds a stealthy, supersonic Batplane, and there are sea-level moorings for a Batboat that doubles as a submarine. And let's not forget Batman's armor-plated, jet-propelled Batmobile!

Batboat

Batmobile

BAT DATA

• The Batcave's Trophy Room holds unique mementos of Batman's career.

• One display case features the costume of the Gray Ghost, young Bruce's favorite TV crimefighter.

• The Batcave's video surveillance system permits Batman to watch over most of Gotham City.

TRAINING EQUIPMENT

The Batcave's well-stocked gymnasium includes tightropes, targets, and tumbling mats among its fighting facilities. Here, Batman, Nightwing, and Robin hone their super-hero skills!

NIGHTWING

Like Bruce Wayne, young circus acrobat Dick Grayson was also tragically orphaned. When Bruce Wayne offered Dick the opportunity to become Robin the Boy Wonder and avenge his parents' deaths, Dick jumped at the chance! Years later, the Boy Wonder grew up to fly solo as nocturnal crime-fighter Nightwing!

Nightwing's emblem is inspired by the winged totem of the "Invisibles" tribe.

THE DYNAMIC DUO broke up when Batman refused to treat Dick as an adult. Reluctantly, Dick left his Robin costume behind in the Batcave.

FIRST COSTUME

Nightwing's costume was a gift from Himalayan mystics. They traded their secret of flight for Dick's help in finding a stolen statue.

NEW WINGS

Dick traveled the world while he did some serious soul-searching and sharpened his fighting skills under new teachers. In Brazil, he learned stealth techniques from a tribe known as the "Invisibles."

CLAYFACE found out the hard way that Gotham's Dynamic Duo is now a Titanic Trio! Returning to Gotham, Dick became Nightwing and now aids Batman and a new Robin in combating crime!

Clayface's silica-based super-conducting mud body is shocked silly!

HIGHWIRE artist Dick Grayson occasionally returns to the big top and performs a death-defying tightrope act with the aerialists of Haley's Circus.

BAT DATA

• **Gangster Tony Zucco murdered Dick's parents, circus stars known as "The Flying Graysons."**

• **Nightwing has his own special Batarangs and detective equipment.**

AERIAL AVENGER

Bruce and Dick mended their friendship, and Batman is happy that his old partner flew home to Gotham to roust rogues like Killer Croc!

ROBIN

Tim Drake was often in trouble... until he saw Batman battling the Joker and decided to be a crusading crimefighter. But when the terrible Two-Face murdered Tim's father, Tim became a real hero as an all-new Robin!

BAD DAD

The lure of easy money was too much for Tim's father, Steven "Shifty" Drake, to resist. "Shifty" was a crook in the employ of Two-Face. When he tried to double-cross the gang boss, Two-Face permanently terminated him.

BAT DATA

• After Dick Grayson, Tim is Bruce Wayne's second ward. He now lives at Wayne Manor.

• Tim attends junior high school in Gotham, and he is also privately tutored by Alfred.

TWO-FACE took vicious revenge when Tim's father betrayed him. The criminal mastermind kidnapped Tim and threatened to drown him in Gotham Harbor! Fortunately, Tim's hero, Batman, leaped to the rescue!

BAT BUDDY

Batman saved Tim from Two-Face but suffered serious injuries. To aid Batman, Tim set the Batboat on auto-pilot and stowed away on board. Back at the Batcave, Tim learned all of Batman's secrets. Tim also discovered Dick Grayson's Robin costume and made it his own!

HELPING THE BAT

Tim Drake is a computer whiz with a knack for Internet sleuthing. While Batman searches for physical clues, Robin downloads vital electronic evidence.

FISTS FLYING, Robin powers into action as the Dark Knight's newest crime-fighting partner. Tim is bold and fearless. These traits are admirable, but sometimes make him act a little recklessly…

ALFRED

Valet Alfred Pennyworth was the first person to know Batman's stunning secret. When Thomas and Martha Wayne were murdered, their faithful butler became Bruce's confidant. Alfred attended to the young orphan's every need so that Bruce could seek his Dark Knight destiny and one day avenge the Waynes' deaths.

A SPOT OF TEA?

Batman, Nightwing, and the entire Bat-Family know that Alfred anxiously awaits their safe return each night from their perilous patrols in Gotham City. More often than not, ever-patient Alfred is ready to offer hot refreshments with a side order of wise counsel.

PATCHING UP Bruce's wounds is Alfred's least-favorite duty. He only wishes he could heal the mental scars inflicted when Bruce's parents died all those years ago.

BAT DATA

• A stage-trained actor, Alfred especially loves the plays of William Shakespeare.

• In his youth, Alfred served in the British Secret Service combating enemy spies.

CAVE KEEPER

Despite his old-fashioned appearance, Alfred is very mechanically inclined. He makes sure that the Batcave's equipment is in tiptop shape. He uses Bruce's secret passwords to access the Batcomputer's databases.

ALFRED IN TROUBLE

Alfred usually keeps the home fires burning at Wayne Manor and the Batcave while the Dark Knight engages evil elsewhere. Occasionally, rogues like Poison Ivy strike at social functions attended by Alfred and his employer. At these times, Alfred is prepared to tangle with a crushing creeper to give Bruce Wayne time to become Batman!

CATCHING THE JOKER tunneling into the Batcave, Alfred clobbered the Clown Prince of Crime with a silver serving tray!

FOOLING FELONS is easy for Alfred, who uses tricks taught him by Batman to slip his bonds. After throwing his voice to fool a criminal, Alfred subdues the astonished would-be kidnapper with his own handcuffs!

COMMISSIONER GORDON

P olice Commissioner James Gordon is Batman's best friend in the war on crime. At first, Gordon was reluctant to work with a mysterious masked vigilante like the Dark Knight. However, he soon realized that he needed some heroic help to clean up Gotham's mean streets!

JIM GORDON isn't afraid to knuckle-dust some no-good hoods! He is very fit for his age and still fights the good fight.

ACTION MAN

Commissioner Gordon is the most honest cop in Gotham City. Fellow officers Harvey Bullock and Renee Montoya look up to their boss, who always leads the charge to root out crime.

BAT DATA

• Although he would trust Batman with his life, Gordon still does not know the Dark Knight's secret identity.

• Gordon contacts the Caped Crusader with the Bat-Signal, a high-powered skylight situated on the roof of G.C.P.D. headquarters!

BATGIRL

Barbara Gordon inherited her father's bravery and dedication to justice… as well as a respect for Batman! At first, Babs donned her own Bat-Costume to clear the Commissioner's name for a crime he didn't commit. Now she uses her own impressive martial-arts skills to fight as Batgirl alongside the Dark Knight.

SECRET LIFE

As Batgirl, Barbara continues to thwart injustice in Gotham with Batman as her masked mentor. Commissioner Gordon, however, has no idea that his daughter leads a secret life! Babs hopes to tell him someday, when the time is right.

BAT DATA

- Many of Batman's foes think Barbara is his daughter!

- Barbara is romantically involved with Dick Grayson, otherwise known as Nightwing!

ROUGHING UP the Riddler is just one of Batgirl's many nightly duties as a member of the Bat-Family. Early on, Batman figured out Batgirl's true identity. Barbara persuaded him not to reveal this truth to her father, Commissioner Gordon.

CITIZENS OF GOTHAM

Most of Gotham City's inhabitants believe Batman is just an "urban legend"—a story made up to frighten criminals. But those who have come face to face with the Caped Crusader know he is Gotham's dedicated defender and that the city would be an even darker place without its Dark Knight!

POLICE HEADQUARTERS is always abuzz with activity in crime-filled Gotham City!

BAT DATA

• Gotham City is a center for international trade—and a haven for crime and criminals on the run!

• The various companies comprising Wayne Enterprises employ a large portion of Gotham's workforce.

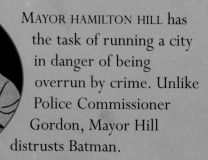

MAYOR HAMILTON HILL has the task of running a city in danger of being overrun by crime. Unlike Police Commissioner Gordon, Mayor Hill distrusts Batman.

SUMMER GLEASON is a reporter for the popular *Gotham Insider* television news magazine. Summer's investigations have led to her abduction by several of Batman's foes. Nevertheless, she is still first on the scene when there's news relating to the Dark Knight!

HARVEY BULLOCK is the G.C.P.D.'s rudest and most rumpled cop. He thinks the Dark Knight is a menace… but that hasn't stopped Harvey from teaming up with him to keep Gotham safe!

ARKHAM

Arkham Asylum is on the spooky outskirts of town. Here, deranged desperados like the Joker, Poison Ivy, and Two-Face are kept under lock and key. Dr. Joan Leland (pictured) is one of several staff psychologists working to rehabilitate these ruthless rogues.

RENEE MONTOYA is a promising young police officer. She frequently partners Det. Harvey Bullock. Much to his annoyance, she has great respect for Batman and his allies.

The G.C.P.D.'s squad cars are no match for the Batmobile.

Officer Montoya shares a clue with Batgirl!

The Joker's mouth is permanently pulled back into a leering, ghoulish grin!

THE JOKER

Don't let his smile fool you! The Ace of Knaves is no laughing matter. Once he was a wiseguy named Jack Napier. But after a dip in a vat of chemicals, Napier got a major makeover! The acids bleached his skin white and dyed his hair green. He emerged as the Clown Prince of Crime, the Joker!

OLD ENEMIES

Batman himself chased Jack Napier through the chemical plant where the Joker was born. Because of that, this jugular-choking jester is determined to destroy the Dark Knight!

3 BALLS 75¢

SULPHURIC ACID

BATTER UP!

The Joker takes delight in devising diabolical death-traps! Reporter Summer Gleason trembles helplessly with fear as Batman swings his fists to save her from striking out for good in the Joker's deadly dissolving dunking booth!

BAT DATA

- The trick flower pinned to the Joker's lapel squirts lethal acid!

- The Joker has spent more time in Arkham Asylum than any other member of Batman's Rogues Gallery. Sadly, it seems he's just a hopeless case!

LAUGH 'TIL IT HURTS

Calculating and cruel, the Joker gets his jollies by inflicting pain! Batman saved Commissioner Gordon from the Joker's drilling dentistry… only to find himself chained to an even more diabolical trap!

BIG PLANS mean big laughs for the Joker. Each of his crimes is more complex and cunning than the previous plot. Here he schemes Gotham's last laugh by scrambling radar signals in order to crash planes!

HARLEY QUINN

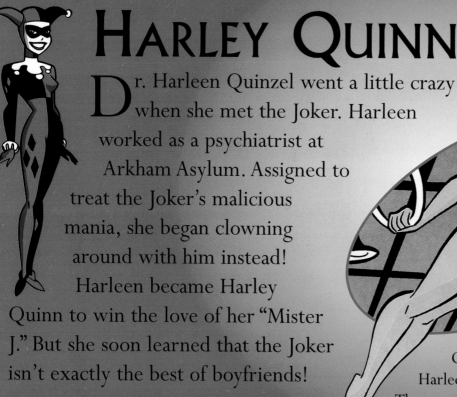

Dr. Harleen Quinzel went a little crazy when she met the Joker. Harleen worked as a psychiatrist at Arkham Asylum. Assigned to treat the Joker's malicious mania, she began clowning around with him instead! Harleen became Harley Quinn to win the love of her "Mister J." But she soon learned that the Joker isn't exactly the best of boyfriends!

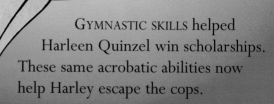

GYMNASTIC SKILLS helped Harleen Quinzel win scholarships. These same acrobatic abilities now help Harley escape the cops.

SOB STORIES

Harleen first treated the Joker's mental illness with clinical detachment. But by telling tragic tales of his childhood, the manipulative Clown Prince of Crime made Harley feel sorry for him. Soon, her pity had turned to passion!

DOMESTIC BLISS

Harley's best-laid plans for dinner and a quiet night at home are interrupted by the Joker's latest criminal caper! Unfortunately, heartless Mister J. would rather grab some take-out while on the lam from the law than sample Harley's home cooking in their Ha-Hacienda hideout!

A WACKY SCHEME to cheer up Mister J. was nearly the death of Batman! Harley figured out that the hungry mouths of piranha normally look like frowns. But, turned upside-down, as Batman was here, the man-eating fish had toothy grins instead!

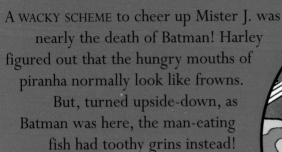

Harley wears white makeup and a jester's costume to win Joker's love.

BAT DATA

• Harley's best friend is fellow femme fatale Pamela Isley, otherwise known as Poison Ivy!

• Harley's certainly no pushover and she sometimes shows her Mister J. a little "tough love" of her own to make up for the Joker's mischievous mistreatment.

HARLEY'S "BABIES" are her twin hyenas. They're laughingly loyal to Harley, but *seriously snarling* whenever the Dark Knight appears!

MAD LOVE

Harley has a love-hate relationship with Mister J. She loves him, but he hates her! Harley keeps working on her comic routines—she knows that *humor* is the way to the Joker's heart.

TWO-FACE

Once, the Dark Knight and Gotham's District Attorney Harvey Dent were equal partners in the war on crime. Although Dent had a temper, the Dark Knight never realized the D.A. had a dark side. Harvey's personality permanently split when an explosion deformed his face. From then on, Dent was a man torn between good and evil as Two-Face!

LUCKY COIN

Dent's two-headed silver dollar has special meaning. Two-Face scarred one side of it and flips it to make decisions for good or ill.

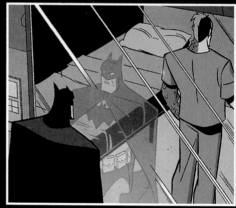

THE DARK KNIGHT visits Two-Face's Arkham cell hoping to find some way of reforming him.

DEADLY CHOICES are made when confronting Two-Face! Dent divides heroes with a coin-toss. While Nightwing saves a child, Robin must defuse a deadly bomb!

PING!

TWO-FACE'S TASTE in clothes reflects his double-sided personality. But, more often than not, Two-Face's *evil* side wins out over his good one!

CRUEL QUIP

Harvey's mental state may be a result of his cruel father. In Mr. Dent's eyes, Harvey was never more than "half a man."

STOP THAT CAR!

With his evil side dominating, a fleeing Two-Face tries to shake the Dark Knight off his getaway car. A flip of Harvey Dent's two-headed silver dollar will decide if Batman remains a hood ornament… or becomes roadkill on Gotham's littered streets!

BAT DATA

• No matter what, Harvey lets his lucky coin decide his actions, even if it means sparing Batman from a bullet!

• Because of his split personality, Two-Face plans all his crimes around the number two.

CATWOMAN

Gotham's best-known cat-burglar, Selina Kyle is the only thief to ever steal Batman's heart! Catwoman once stole from the rich to fund a nature reserve for mountain lions and she is more mischievous than malicious. Batman just hopes she doesn't use up all of her nine lives too soon.

CAT LOVER

Selina loves felines of all kinds. Trained jungle cats occasionally help her out, and the proceeds of her robberies often go to cat-saving charities.

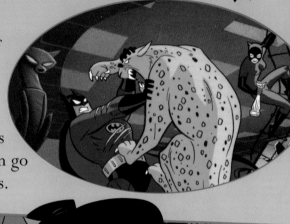

PERPETUALLY PURSUED by Batman, Catwoman usually claws her way to freedom. Sometimes she lets him catch her... hoping to learn his identity!

JOINING FORCES, Batman and Catwoman have battled terrorists and halted an animal outbreak that drove Gotham's pets crazy!

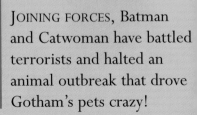

CAT CRADLED

Catwoman was overcome by exhaustion and bitter cold while on a snowy mission with Batman. To stop Selina freezing to death, Batman cloaked her in his insulated cape.

When her feminine charms don't work, this feline fatale uses a cat-o'-nine tails to slip free from Batman!

BAT DATA

• Bruce Wayne sometimes dreams he is happily married to Selina.

• Catwoman just can't keep her paws off flashy jewels!

• Like a cat, Selina is extremely agile and always lands on her feet.

THE CAT AND THE BAT

Batman knows Selina isn't *truly* evil. If she reformed, Catwoman could be an invaluable ally, and Gotham's nights would also be less lonely for the Dark Knight. But a leopard can't change its spots. And Catwoman, for now, seems reluctant to give up her thieving ways.

POISON IVY

Botanist Pamela Isley has always looked her best in green. She was born immune to the poisonous plants that she loves. In fact, her dangerous experiments with lethal leaves gave her a toxic touch! Before long, shy, shrinking violet Pamela Isley had sprouted into bewitching beauty Poison Ivy!

IVY BLOOMED with menace when she tried to kill her fiancé, Gotham's D.A. Harvey Dent, for plowing up a field of flowers to build a prison.

JUST ONE KISS

Ivy has complete control over all of the flowery scents and toxins her body emits. When imprisoned in Arkham Asylum, she is kept safely behind Plexiglas. Men are very susceptible to her cunning charms and lethal lips.

BAT DATA

- Like her beloved plants, Ivy thrives in sunlight and fertile soil.

- Ivy is committed to preserving Earth's plant life… at all costs!

- Pamela was once engaged to Harvey Dent, alias the psycho-villain Two-Face!

BAT'S FOR DINNER

Beware: these plants are hungry...
A stroll through Poison Ivy's
botanical gardens certainly isn't a
walk in the park! While attempting
to ensnare Ivy, the Dark Knight
almost became an appetizing
Bat-snack for Poison Ivy's giant
man-eating Venus Flytrap!

POISON TOYS

Poison Ivy sometimes wears thorny
rings to prick unsuspecting victims!
Ivy's arsenal of weapons also
includes fast-growing seeds and
spores that germinate into strangling
stems and feasting flytraps!

VILE VINES
threaten to
choke Batman
with their thorny
brambles. Always
prepared, the Dark
Knight's Utility Belt
includes a spray to wither
these wicked weeds!

PENGUIN

Oswald Cobblepot has a waddling walk and a beak-like nose. He prefers to wear a tuxedo, but he's no gentleman, nor is he as harmless as the flightless fowl he resembles. For in Gotham City, the Penguin is a criminal "fixer," whose Iceberg Lounge nightclub conceals a nest of smuggling and sin!

SNEAKY SABOTAGE

The Penguin once discovered the identity of the man who serviced the Batmobile! After learning that Earl Cooper was the mechanic who built Batman's vigilante vehicle, Cobblepot set out to sabotage the jet-powered car!

UMBRELLAS are the Penguin's favorite weapons. One may conceal a gun, another a flame-thrower!

"BIRDS OF A FEATHER flock together," or so they say. The Penguin hatches all of his criminal schemes around them!

BAT DATA

• **The Penguin has few fighting skills and is no match for Batman.**

• **He generally surrounds himself with hired muscle.**

• **Cobblepot's Iceberg Lounge is the *coolest* hot spot in Gotham City!**

KILLER CROC

Pro-wrestler "Killer Croc" Morgan was hungry for revenge when he escaped jail and swam to Gotham City. He was looking for Harvey Bullock, the cop who imprisoned him. But the ferocious freak didn't count on having to fight a knockdown, drag-out bout with Batman.

THE CHAMP

Killer Croc began his career as a sideshow attraction. His reptilian appearance frightened carnival crowds as he clawed his way to a wrestling championship. But the money-hungry Croc soon turned to crime and was sent to jail by G.C.P.D. Detective Harvey Bullock!

ON THE RUN, Croc found refuge with fellow freaks. Batman found the menacing Morgan planning to steal from the retired circus performers who had welcomed him into their family.

RĀ'S AL GHŪL

Roughly translated, his name means "The Demon's Head" in Arabic. Immortal international terrorist Rā's al Ghūl owes his longevity to the frothy Lazarus Pits. Like the mythical fountain of youth, these bubbling baths have kept Rā's alive for countless centuries. In all that time he has pursued one objective: to conquer Earth and restore it to paradise! But at what cost?

ECO-TERRORIST

Rā's al Ghūl will do anything to rid the planet of pollution and pestilence. Unfortunately, that often means drastically reducing Earth's human population! Batman has sworn to stop this eco-terror!

UBU, Rā's's bodyguard, never leaves his side. Ubu's strength is considerable, but Batman knows he is slow-witted and easy to defeat!

DADDY'S GIRL Talia does not always agree with her father's malicious methods but is utterly loyal to Rā's al Ghūl and his cause.

TALIA

She is known as "The Daughter of the Demon." Talia teamed up with Batman to investigate a robbery from Bruce's company, WayneTech, carried out by the Society of Shadows. In truth, Talia planned to double-cross the Dark Knight, but instead she fell in love with him!

UNREQUITED LOVE

Rā's al Ghūl was so impressed with Batman's strength and intelligence that he schemed to force the Dark Knight into marrying Talia! Bruce and Talia already share a mutual affection. However, Talia's allegiance to Rā's always comes between their love.

DEADLY BEAUTY Talia was schooled in martial arts by Rā's al Ghūl. When on missions, she carries a pistol loaded with knockout tranquilizer darts.

BATTLING BATGIRL and the rest of the Bat-Family continues to be Talia's fate. As long as she shares her father's dreams of conquest, she remains on the wrong side of the law!

MAD HATTER

At first, awkward and shy Jervis Tetch only wanted his co-worker Alice to return his love. But when she wouldn't, the insanely jealous scientist used his experimental mind-controlling circuitry to *make* poor Alice fall in love with him. Calling himself the Mad Hatter, Tetch then tried to take over all Gotham!

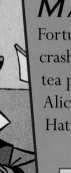

MADMAN

Fortunately, Batman crashed Tetch's twisted tea party and set helpless Alice free from the Mad Hatter's hypnotic clutches!

STRONG-WILLED Batman must shield his mask and cowl against the effects of the Mad Hatter's brain-blasting machinery.

IN HIS WILDEST DREAMS, Jervis wishes beautiful Alice were his bride and they were living among the friendly freaks of Wonderland!

BAT DATA

• The Mad Hatter blames Batman for the loss of his beloved Alice.

• Tetch once hid micro-circuitry inside native dolls from Central America in order to take over the minds of Gotham City's wealthiest citizens!

SCARECROW

Jonathan Crane delighted in frightening people and animals. He furthered his scary studies as a professor of Subliminal Psychology at Gotham University. When Crane's colleagues had him fired because of his disturbing experiments, the psychotic professor vowed vengeance by becoming the fearful Scarecrow!

BAT DATA

• Crane's Fear Toxin makes victims experience their worst terrors!

• The Scarecrow also has a secret fear—of Batman!

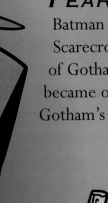

FEAR FOE

Batman foiled the Scarecrow's revenge on the staff of Gotham University. However, Crane became one of his most frightful foes, targeting Gotham's citizens with his Fear Toxin.

RAGGED ROGUE

Scarecrow resembles a gangly and gruesome ghoul. His creepy costume even includes a frayed hangman's noose looped around his neck!

MR. FREEZE

Victor Fries is an expert in cryogenics, the study of suspended animation. Fries used his knowledge to save his ill wife, Nora. Fries's employer, Gothcorp, wanted to pull the plug on her treatment. But when Fries tried to stop Gothcorp, he was bathed in super-coolants. The accident turned him into cold-hearted Mr. Freeze!

BAT DATA

• Fries risks death if his altered body chemistry rises above the freezing point of water.

• Mr. Freeze's cold heart can only be thawed by the love of Nora Fries.

ICE GUN

Mr. Freeze wields a weapon that can chill Batman to the bone! Freeze's cryo-gun creates slippery sheaths of snow. It can also encase the Dark Knight in a man-sized iceberg!

Air-conditioning units keep Mr. Freeze ice-cool.

MR. FREEZE'S body armor includes air-conditioning units to keep his body icy-cool.

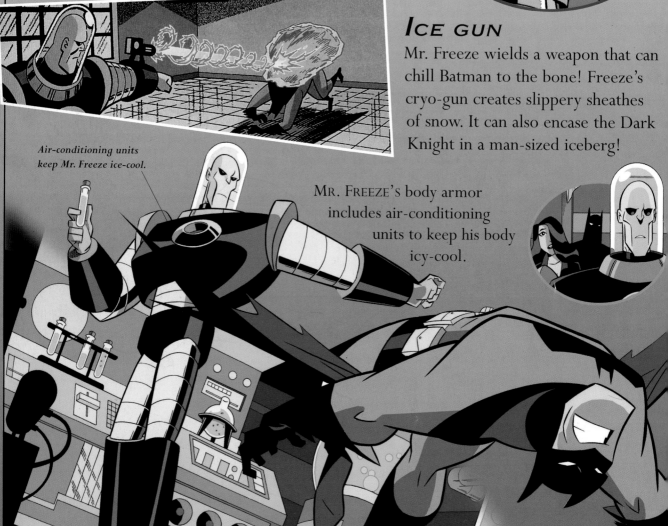

CLAYFACE

Matt Hagen's name was mud in the acting world after he scarred his handsome face in a car crash. A new career beckoned when ruthless businessman Roland Daggett gave him a special skin cream. With it, Hagen could reshape his features like clay! Little did he realize that the ointment would mold him into a monster!

DAGGETT'S MEN made Hagen consume gallons of the ointment! The stuff altered Hagen's body chemistry and turned him into a man of mud!

FEET OF CLAY

After absorbing the experimental cream, Hagen could morph his entire body into any shape he could imagine. In his new role as Clayface, he took on Daggett and Gotham's Dark Knight Detective!

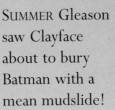

SUMMER Gleason saw Clayface about to bury Batman with a mean mudslide!

BAT DATA

• No longer human, Matt Hagen is now composed entirely of muddy clay.

• Clayface once created a clay lady friend for himself out of his own body!

MASK OF THE PHANTASM

Andrea Beaumont was Bruce Wayne's fiancée, but she gave back his ring and broke his heart. Bruce didn't know that criminal connections had forced Andrea and her father to flee Gotham City. Soon Bruce would have to choose between his lost love and his solemn vow to uphold the law!

With a sharp scythe, the Phantasm was a grim reaper indeed!

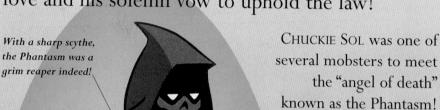

CHUCKIE SOL was one of several mobsters to meet the "angel of death" known as the Phantasm!

MASKED AVENGER

Andrea's father, Carl, made a big mistake getting mixed up with gangsters. But the mysterious Phantasm took revenge on the criminals who sent Carl to an early grave!

WHEN BRUCE first met Andrea, he was still struggling to find a way to avenge his parents' deaths. Her love briefly helped him forget his burning need for justice.

JIM GORDON was sure Batman was not to blame for the mobster murders. But *who* was?

JOKER IN THE PACK

Strangely, the Clown Prince of Crime shared a connection with Bruce and Andrea. Before he became the jeering Joker, he was one of the Gotham goons who had criminal links to Carl Beaumont!

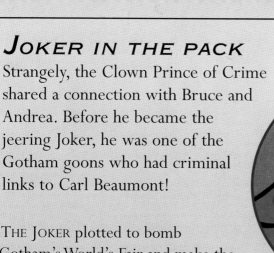

THE JOKER plotted to bomb Gotham's World's Fair and make the Phantasm a *real* ghost! Andrea threw off her mask and saved Bruce, but she and the Joker were apparently blown to bits.

BRUCE'S HEART was broken all over again when Andrea gave her life to save him. In the shadows of the Batcave, Alfred offered some comforting words.

BAT DATA

• Bruce asked Andrea to marry him on a moonlit Gotham beach.

• Andrea was schooled in martial arts and could match Bruce kick for kick!

SHADOW OF THE PHANTASM

Andrea Beaumont's avenging alter ego crossed a line that the Dark Knight refuses to go beyond: no matter how serious the crime, Batman would *never* take a life to achieve justice.

THE RIDDLER

Edward Nygma turned his love of riddles and puzzles into a career as a video-game designer. His *Riddle of the Minotaur* game made millions of dollars for its manufacturer, Competitron. But Nygma received nothing! He took his revenge by becoming the Riddler, a villain who leaves cryptic clues to his crimes!

Edward Nygma (*or E. Nygma, get it?*) plans all his criminal capers around puns or puzzles.

CLUEMASTER

The Riddler once gave up crime and became a celebrity spokesman for the Wacko Toy Company. But Nygma still longed to beat Batman just once in a game of wits. He was even willing to forsake fame and fortune for it! The Riddler resumed his criminal career… and Batman still outsmarted him!

BAT DATA

• The Riddler's question-mark cane can be a shocking weapon!

• The Riddler won't commit a crime unless he first sends a clue to Batman.

• Nygma once kidnapped Commissioner Gordon and hid him inside a video game!

BANE

Crime boss Rupert Thorne hired muscle-man Bane to body-slam Batman right out of Gotham! Bane proved he was the right man for the job by kicking Killer Croc's tail before challenging the Dark Knight himself. Little did Batman know that Bane was pumped up with a muscle-making steroid known as Venom!

THORNE learned the hard way that it's a very bad idea to double-cross Bane!

FIGHTING FIT

Fueled by Venom, Bane's a muscle-bound mauler! That's why Batman was forced to yank out Bane's steroid tubes in order to sap his strength!

PENA DURO prison was once Bane's home. Bane escaped and left behind any friends he may have had there.

MAN-BAT

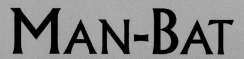

Zoologist Kirk Langstrom should have known better than to inject himself with his own special bat-extract serum. The formula made him go "batty"—literally! The normally nice scientist was transformed into a terrifying, rampaging, leathery-winged Man-Bat!

FRANCINE

Kirk's wife Francine was also a bat expert. She prayed that her love for Kirk would reach his human side before it was too late!

THANKS TO Batman, Kirk was restored to normal… but he could change back any time!

AT FIRST, Batman battled the crazed creature.

KNOCKOUT gas helped Batman soothe the savage beast!

BAT DATA

• Man-Bat uses sonar-like echolocation to fly in the pitch dark and capture his prey.

• Francine once tried Kirk's serum and turned into a She-Bat!

VENTRILOQUIST

Arnold Wesker is just a poor pathetic puppet to the evil Scarface. But Scarface is the *real* puppet, a wooden dummy with a life of his own! Timid Arnold hears voices in his head. And the one he listens to most belongs to Scarface. The little criminal is always the one pulling the strings!

CRUEL MASTER

Arnold is meek and mild-mannered. He wouldn't harm a fly. Scarface, on the other hand, is violent, vengeful, and utterly villainous. Sadly, neither one can live without the other!

DEADLY DOLL Scarface opened up with his pint-sized Tommy gun— and the Dynamic Duo dived for cover as the bullets flew!

ARNOLD once thought he was free from Scarface. But the dummy's influence was too strong for him.

BAT DATA

• Scarface has his own gang who answer to *him*, not Arnold.

• Scarface wants to take over Gotham City's criminal underworld.

ROGUES' GALLERY

Batman's evil enemies aren't just limited to the sinister supervillains of Arkham Asylum. Unfortunately, the Dark Knight's Rogues' Gallery also includes a gaggle of Gotham gangsters, criminal civilians with insane intentions, and malicious mercenaries who'll do *anything* for a fast buck.

GUN GOONS

Gotham is filled with hoodlums and thugs. These wiseguys work for organized crime families, or serve as "hired help" to costumed crooks like the Penguin or Scarecrow.

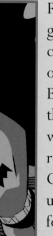

RED CLAW is a global terrorist who cares only for her own wealth. Batman first met this vicious vixen when she plotted to release a plague in Gotham City unless paid a fortune.

SENSEI

Batman traveled the world to learn crucial combat disciplines. In the process, he also made many enemies determined to test the Dark Knight's martial-arts mettle. Some of these foes include the Ninja (a.k.a. Kyodai Ken) and the Sensei (left), leader of the lawless League of Assassins .

WHACK!

HUGO STRANGE

This sinister mind-doctor succeeded where other villains couldn't… he discovered the Dark Knight's identity! With blackmail in mind, Strange used his invention to read Bruce Wayne's thoughts, and threatened to sell his secret to the highest bidder!

RUPERT THORNE defeated all rival gang bosses, including the infamous Arnold Stromwell, to claim control over Gotham City's underworld. Cunning and cruel, he has repeatedly tried to terminate Batman.

MAXIE ZEUS thinks he's the father of the Greek gods. Maxie's madness made him ruler of a Gotham criminal empire. Like mythical Zeus, he hurls lightning at his enemies with electrifying weaponry. Or, as Batman learned, he's just as likely to throw them to the lions!

GAZETTEER

Alfred Pennyworth (voiced by Clive Revill and Efrem Zimbalist Jr.)
First appeared in THE CAT AND THE CLAW, Part One (Episode #1).

Bane (voiced by Henry Silva)
First appeared in BANE (Episode #71).

Batgirl (voiced by Melissa Gilbert and Tara Charendoff)
Barbara Gordon first appeared in HEART OF STEEL, Part One (Episode #39).
First appeared as Batgirl in SHADOW OF THE BAT, Part One (Episode #61).

Batman (voiced by Kevin Conroy)
First appeared in THE CAT AND THE CLAW, Part One (Episode #1).

Catwoman (voiced by Adrienne Barbeau)
First appeared in THE CAT AND THE CLAW Part One (Episode #1).

Clayface (voiced by Ron Perlman)
First appeared in FEAT OF CLAY, Part One (Episode #4).

Commissioner Gordon (voiced by Bob Hastings)
First appeared in THE CAT AND THE CLAW, Part One (Episode #1).

Harley Quinn (voiced by Arlene Sorkin)
First appeared in JOKER'S FAVOR (Episode #7).

Harvey Bullock (voiced by Robert Costanza)
First appeared in ON LEATHER WINGS (Episode #2).

Hugo Strange (voiced by Ray Buktenica)
First appeared in THE STRANGE SECRET OF BRUCE WAYNE (Episode #29).

Joan Leland (voiced by Suzanne Stone)
First appeared in HARLEY'S HOLIDAY (Episode #76).

Joker (voiced by Mark Hamill)
First appeared in JOKER'S FAVOR (Episode #7).

Killer Croc (voiced by Aron Kincaid)
First appeared in VENDETTA (Episode #21).

Mad Hatter (voiced by Roddy McDowall)
First appeared in MAD AS A HATTER (Episode #24).

Man-Bat (voiced by by Marc Singer)
First appeared in ON LEATHER WINGS (Episode #2).

Maxie Zeus (voiced by Steve Suskind)
First appeared in FIRE FROM OLYMPUS (Episode #60).

Mayor Hamilton Hill (voiced by Lloyd Bochner)
First appeared in ON LEATHER WINGS (Episode #2).

Mr. Freeze (voiced by Michael Ansara)
First appeared in in the Emmy Award-winning HEART OF ICE (Episode #3).

Nightwing (voiced by Loren Lester)
Dick Grayson's origins as Robin are chronicled in the two-part ROBIN'S RECKONING (Episodes #51 and #53).

Penguin (voiced by Paul Williams)
First appeared in I'VE GOT BATMAN IN MY BASEMENT (Episode #20).

Phantasm (voiced by Dana Delaney)
First appeared in the feature-length MASK OF THE PHANTASM.

Poison Ivy (voiced by Diane Pershing)
First appeared in PRETTY POISON (Episode #9).

Rā's al Ghūl (voiced by David Warner)
First appeared in OFF BALANCE (Episode #44).

Red Claw (voiced by Kate Mulgrew)
First appeared in THE CAT AND THE CLAW, Part One (Episode #1).

Renee Montoya (voiced by Ingrid Oliu and Liane Schirmer)
First appeared in PRETTY POISON (Episode #9).

Riddler (voiced by John Glover)
First appeared in IF YOU'RE SO SMART, WHY AREN'T YOU RICH? (Episode #41).

Robin (voiced by Matt Valencia)
Tim Drake first donned the costume of Robin in SINS OF THE FATHER (Episode #87).

Rupert Thorne (voiced by John Vernon)
First appeared in TWO-FACE, Part One (Episode #17).

Scarecrow (voiced by Henry Polic II and Jeffrey Combs)
First appeared in NOTHING TO FEAR (Episode #10).

Summer Gleason (voiced by Mari Devon)
First appeared in CHRISTMAS WITH THE JOKER (Episode #38).

Talia Head (voiced by Helen Slater)
First appeared in OFF BALANCE (Episode #44).

Two-Face (voiced by Richard Moll)
D.A. Harvey Dent first appeared in ON LEATHER WINGS (Episode #2). Harvey turned to evil in the two-part TWO-FACE (Episodes #17 and #18).

Ventriloquist and Scarface (voiced by George Dzundza)
First appeared in READ MY LIPS (Episode #59).

INDEX

A

Alice 34
Arkham Asylum 19, 21, 24, 28

B

Bane (Rupert Thorne) **41**
Batarangs 6, 11
Batboat 9, 13
Batcave **8-9**, 15
Batcycles 9
Batgirl (Barbara Gordon) **17**, 19, 33
Batmobile 9
Batplane 9
Bat-Signal 16
Beaumont, Andrea 38, 39
Bullock, Det. Harvey 16, 19, 31

C, D

Catwoman (Selina Kyle) **26-27**
Clayface (Matt Hagen) 11, **37**
Cooper, Earl 30
Daggett, Roland 37

G, H

Gleason, Summer 19, 37
Gordon, Commissioner Jim **16**, 17, 18, 21, 38, 40
Gotham City **18-19**
Gothcorp 36
Hill, Mayor Hamilton 18

J, K, L

Joker (Jack Napier) 15, 19, **20-21**, 22, 23, 39
Killer Croc 11, **31**, 41
Leland, Dr. Joan 19

M

Mad Hatter (Jervis Tetch) **34**
Man-Bat (Kirk Langstrom) **42**
Mask of the Phantasm **38-39**
Montoya, Renee 16, 19
Mr. Freeze (Victor Fries) **36**

N

Nightwing (Dick Grayson) **10-11**, 14, 17, 24
Ninja (Kyodai Ken) 44

P, Q

Penguin (Oswald Cobblepot) **30**
Pennyworth, Alfred 8, **14-15**, 39
Poison Ivy (Pamela Isley) 15, 19, **28-29**
Quinn, Harley (Dr. Harleen Quinzel) **22-23**

R

Rā's al Ghūl **32**, 33
Red Claw 15, 44
Riddler (Edward Nygma) 17, **40**
Robin (Dick Grayson) 10
Robin (Tim Drake) **12-13**, 24

S

Scarecrow (Jonathan Crane) **35**
Scarface 43
Sensei 44
Society of Shadows 33
Sol, Chuckie 38
Strange, Dr. Hugo 45

T

Talia 32, **33**
Thorne, Rupert 41
Training Equipment 9
Two-Face (Harvey Dent) 12, 13, 19, **24-25**, 29

U, V

Ubu 32
Utility Belt 7
Ventriloquist (Arnold Wesker) **43**

W, Z

Wayne Enterprises 6, 18
Wayne Manor 8, 11, 15
WayneTech 33
Zeus, Maxie 45
Zucco, Tony

ACKNOWLEDGMENTS

Dorling Kindersley would like to thank the following DC artists for their contributions to this book:

Terry Austin; Terry Beatty; Rick Burchett; Dan Davis; Bo Hampton; Brandon Kruse; Rob Leigh; Tim Levins; Mike Parobeck; Brad Rader; Craig Rousseau; Joe Staton; Bruce Timm; Stan Woch.

The author would like to gratefully thank:
Steve Korté, Alastair Dougall, Robert Perry, Shaun McLaughlin,
Kevin Kiniry, and Jennifer Myskowski.

Dorling Kindersley would like to thank:
Steve Korté and James Gardner at DC Comics.
Julia March for editorial assistance.